PRE-APPRENTICESHIP
MATHS & LITERACY FOR
HORTICULTURE

Graduated exercises and practice exam

Andrew Spencer

NELSON
A Cengage Company

A+ National Pre-apprenticeship Maths & Literacy for Horticulture
1st Edition
Andrew Spencer

Publishing editor: Sarah Broomhall
Project editor: Aynslie Harper
Proofreader: Katharine Day
Text designer: Miranda Costa
Cover designer: Aisling Gallagher
Cover image: Shutterstock.com/IVL
Permissions researcher: Helen Mammides
Production controller: Emma Roberts
Reprint: Katie McCappin
Typeset by Q2A Media

Any URLs contained in this publication were checked for currency during the production process. Note, however, that the publisher cannot vouch for the ongoing currency of URLs.

For product information and technology assistance,
in Australia call **1300 790 853**;
in New Zealand call **0800 449 725**

For permission to use material from this text or product, please email **aust.permissions@cengage.com**

ISBN 978 0 17 047338 5

Cengage Learning Australia
Level 7, 80 Dorcas Street
South Melbourne, Victoria Australia 3205

Cengage Learning New Zealand
Unit 4B Rosedale Office Park
331 Rosedale Road, Albany, North Shore 0632, NZ

For learning solutions, visit **cengage.com.au**

Printed in Australia by Ligare Pty Limited.
1 2 3 4 5 6 7 26 25 24 23 22

A+ National
PRE-APPRENTICESHIP
Maths & Literacy for Horticulture

Contents

Introduction

It has always been important to understand, from a teacher's perspective, the nature of the mathematical skills students need for their future, rather than teaching them 'textbook mathematics'. This has been a guiding principle behind the development of the content in this workbook. To teach maths that is *relevant* to students seeking apprenticeships is the best that we can do, to give students an education in the field that they would like to work in.

The content in this resource is aimed at the level that is needed for students to have the best possibility of improving their maths and literacy skills specifically for trades. Students can use this workbook to prepare for an apprenticeship entry assessment, or to even assist with basic numeracy and literacy at the VET/TAFE level. Coupled with the activities on the NelsonNet website, https://www.nelsonnet.com.au/free-resources, these resources have the potential to improve the students' understanding of basic mathematical concepts that can be applied to trades. These resources have been trialled, and they work.

Commonly used trade terms are introduced so that students have a basic understanding of terminology that they will encounter in the workplace environment. Students who can complete this workbook and reach an 80 per cent or higher outcome in all topics will have achieved the goal of this resource. These students will go on to complete work experience, do a VET accredited course, or will be able to gain entry into VET/TAFE or an apprenticeship in the trade of their choice.

The content in this workbook is the first step to bridging the gap between what has been learnt in previous years, and what needs to be remembered and re-learnt for use in trades. Students will significantly benefit from the consolidation of the basic maths and literacy concepts.

Every school has students who want to work with their hands, and not all students want to go to university. The best students want to learn what they don't already know; and if students want to learn, then this book has the potential to give them a good start in life.

This resource has been specifically tailored to prepare students for sitting apprenticeship or VET/TAFE admission tests, and for giving students the basic skills they will need for a career in trade. In many ways, it is a win–win situation, with students enjoying and studying relevant maths for work, and Trades and Registered Training Officers (RTOs) receiving students who have improved basic maths and literacy skills.

All that is needed from students is patience, hard work, a positive attitude, a belief in themselves that they can do it and a desire to achieve.

About the author

Andrew graduated from SACAE Underdale in 1988 with a Bachelor of Education. In 1989, Andrew went on to attend West Virginia University, where he completed a Master of Science (specialising in teacher education), while lecturing part-time.

In 1993, Andrew moved to NSW and began teaching at Sydney Boys' High, where he taught in a range of subject areas including Mathematics, English, Science, Classics, Physical Education and Technical Studies. His sense of practical mathematics continued to develop with the range of subject areas he taught in.

Andrew moved back to South Australia in 1997 with a diverse knowledge base and an understanding of the importance of using mathematics in different practical subject areas. He began teaching with the De La Salle Brothers in 1997 in South Australia, where he continues to work and teach today. Andrew has worked in collaboration with the SACE Board to help develop resources for mathematics with a practical focus.

In 2011, Andrew was awarded the John Gaffney Mathematics Education Trust Award for valuable contributions to the teaching of Mathematics in South Australia. Andrew received a Recognition of Excellence for outstanding contributions to the teaching profession by CEASA in both 2011 and 2012 and, in 2014, he was one of 12 teachers from across Australia to work in collaboration with the Chief Scientist of Australia to develop a better understanding of the role of mathematics in industry. As part of this role, he undertook research in this area, spent time working with the industry and then fed the results back to the Chief Scientist.

Andrew continues to develop the pre-apprenticeship and vocational titles, based on mathematics and literacy, to assist and support the learning of students who want to follow a vocational career path. He is currently working towards the nineteenth title in this series. The titles have also been adapted in the UK and Asia, as the importance of this type of functional mathematics continues to grow. All schools have students who will follow a vocational pathway and it continues to be a strong focus of Andrew's to support the learning needs of these students.

Acknowledgements

For Paula, Zach, Katelyn, Mum and Dad.

To the De La Salle Brothers for their selfless work with all students.

To Dr Pauline Carter for her unwavering support of all Mathematics teachers.

To all students who value learning, who are willing to work hard and who have character … and are characters!

Unit 1: Spelling

Short-answer questions

Specific instructions to students

- This is an exercise to help you to identify and correct spelling errors.
- Read the activity below and then answer accordingly.

Read the following passage, and identify and correct the spelling errors.

> Carlene is considering making horticulture her carear path. She is very interested in designing different landscapes and working with clients to improve their home landscapes. After researching what gardener's asistants and horticulturalists do, Carlene decides that she would like to look at a project. She comes up with a range of ideas and drafts them on paper. After that, Carlene looks at how to actually plan a living landscape. She finds that there is a searies of stages to be completed as part of the proces.
>
> Carlene sets out an area on paper that she thinks will fit with a cliant's dimentions. Next, she plots out the features that can't change, which includes: buldings, trees, driveways, yard entrances and irigation systems. One thought that comes to Carlene's mind is the role of shade in designing a landscape. Carlene thinks it might be an idea to include a comppass direction in one corner of the paper to remind her of the direction of the sunlight and shadow paterns.
>
> Carlene also thinks it will be good idea to use trasing paper overlays to allow for diferent types of compasitions, paths and propportions. Next, she desides to draw in the type of shrubbs she would like and where they will go. During this time, Carlene is always concious of using a scale and she makes sure that everything is in propartion on her draft.

Incorrect words:

_____

_____

Correct words:

_____

_____

Unit 2: Alphabetising

Short-answer questions

Specific instructions to students

- In this unit, you will be able to practise your alphabetising skills.
- Read the activity below and then answer accordingly.

Put the following words into alphabetical order.

Pruning   Secateurs
Nursery   Chemicals
Groundcover   Wheelbarrow
Fertiliser   Irrigation
Chainsaw   Spray drift

Answer:

_____

_____

_____

_____

_____

_____

_____

_____

_____

_____

iStockphoto/lissart

Read the following passage and answer the questions in full sentences.

A horticulturist is someone who has the ability to use scientific knowledge to cultivate and propagate plants. This knowledge can be used to provide technical information to fruit, vegetable and flower growers and, in some cases, farmers. A horticulturist may undertake pest and disease investigations and consider enhanced varieties of plants that have greater resistance to specific diseases. Landscaping design to create gardens is another task that horticulturalists may be involved in. Horticulturalists may also be involved with recreational areas and parks, and could have a focus of preserving natural resources.

Another focus of a horticulturist could be to carry out plant research, usually within a certain discipline. The role of horticulturalists can be broadened to include studies into plant evolution and development under natural conditions. A plant geneticist undertakes experiments on plants so as to produce new generations of plants through artificial selection. These plants will contain particular qualities that may be specific to certain environments. These types of horticulturists generally use laboratory equipment and multifaceted techniques to study these plants.

A horticulturist could be employed by construction or landscaping companies to design and develop a landscape for a particular site. They grow, cultivate and propagate flowers, a range of grasses, shrubs and trees. Horticulturalists often advise clients on plant products and plan and construct irrigation to assist with maintaining the look and integrity of the greenery. Horticulturists are educated to know the types of plants that could co-exist together and grow successfully. A basic knowledge is needed in the subjects of climate, soil types, the use and application of fundamental nutrients and the care of plants.

Nearly all horticulturists spend time in an office, though being in the field is preferred and compulsory for many. The ability to be able to work with clients, and have open and honest communication, is needed. A horticulturalist may be required to supervise landscapers and gardeners to ensure that the correct operations are being carried out. Planning, budgeting and organising landscaping or gardening projects are common tasks that horticulturalists need to be competent at.

QUESTION 1

What is one important ability that a horticulturalist should have?

Answer:

_____

QUESTION 2

What are some of the tasks that a horticulturalist is involved in?

Answer:

_____

_____

QUESTION 3

What does a plant geneticist do?

Answer:

_____

QUESTION 4

What other basic knowledge does a horticulturalist require?

Answer:

_____

_____

_____

Shutterstock.com/yuris

QUESTION 5

What are some of the tasks that a horticulturalist needs to carry out or be involved with when not in the field?

Answer:

_____

_____

MATHEMATICS

Unit 4: General Mathematics

Specific instructions to students

- This unit is designed to help you to improve your general mathematical skills.
- Read the following questions and answer all of them in the spaces provided.
- You may not use a calculator.
- You need to show all working.

QUESTION 1

What unit of measurement is used to measure:

a the length of a garden bed?

Answer:

_____

b the pressure in a spray backpack?

Answer:

_____

c the amount of mulch for the garden?

Answer:

_____

d the weight of a compost bag?

Answer:

_____

e the speed of a vehicle?

Answer:

_____

f the length of a paver?

Answer:

_____

g the cost of a hose?

Answer:

_____

QUESTION 2

Give examples of how the following might be used in the horticulture industry.

a percentages

Answer:

_____

b decimals

Answer:

_____

c fractions

Answer:

_____

d mixed numbers

Answer:

_____

e ratios

Answer:

_____

f angles

Answer:

_____

QUESTION 3
Convert the following units.

a 1.2 metres to cm and mm

Answer:

b 4 tonne to kg

Answer:

c 260 centimetres to mm

Answer:

d 1140 mL to litres

Answer:

e 1650 g to kilograms

Answer:

f 1.8 kg to grams

Answer:

g 3 metres to cm and mm

Answer:

h 4.5 L to millilitres

Answer:

QUESTION 4
Write the following in descending order.

0.4   0.04   4.1   40.0   400.00   4.0

Answer:

QUESTION 5
Write the decimal number that is between:

a 0.2 and 0.4

Answer:

b 1.8 and 1.9

Answer:

c 12.4 and 12.5

Answer:

d 28.3 and 28.4

Answer:

e 101.5 and 101.7

Answer:

QUESTION 6
Round off the following numbers to two (2) decimal places.

a 12.346

Answer:

b 2.251

Answer:

c 123.897

Answer:

d 688.882

Answer:

e 1209.741

Answer:

9780170473385

QUESTION 7

Estimate the following by approximation.

a $1288 \times 19 =$

Answer:

_____

b $201 \times 20 =$

Answer:

_____

c $497 \times 12.2 =$

Answer:

_____

d $1008 \times 10.3 =$

Answer:

_____

e $399 \times 22 =$

Answer:

_____

f $201 - 19 =$

Answer:

_____

g $502 - 61 =$

Answer:

_____

h $1003 - 49 =$

Answer:

_____

i $10001 - 199 =$

Answer:

_____

j $99.99 - 39.8 =$

Answer:

_____

QUESTION 8

What do the following add up to?

a $4, $4.99 and $144.95

Answer:

_____

b   8.75, 6.9 and 12.55

Answer:

_____

c   650 mm, 1800 mm and 2290 mm

Answer:

_____

d   21.3 mm, 119.8 mm and 884.6 mm

Answer:

_____

QUESTION 9

Subtract the following.

a   2338 from 7117

Answer:

_____

b   1786 from 3112

Answer:

_____

c   5979 from 8014

Answer:

_____

d   11 989 from 26 221

Answer:

_____

e   108 767 from 231 111

Answer:

_____

QUESTION 10

Use division to solve the following.

a $2177 \div 7 =$

Answer:

___

b $4484 \div 4 =$

Answer:

___

c $63.9 \div 0.3 =$

Answer:

___

d $121.63 \div 1.2 =$

Answer:

___

e $466.88 \div 0.8$

Answer:

___

The following information is provided for question 11.

To solve using BODMAS, in order from left to right, solve the **B**rackets first, then **O**f, then **D**ivision, then **M**ultiplication, then **A**ddition and lastly **S**ubtraction. The following example has been done for your reference.

EXAMPLE

Solve $(4 \times 7) \times 2 + 6 - 4$.

STEP 1

Solve the Brackets first: $(4 \times 7) = 28$.

STEP 2

No Division so next solve Multiplication:
$28 \times 2 = 56$.

STEP 3

Addition is next: $56 + 6 = 62$.

STEP 4

Subtraction is the last process: $62 - 4 = 58$.

FINAL ANSWER:

58

QUESTION 11

Use BODMAS to solve the following.

a $(6 \times 9) \times 5 + 7 - 2 =$

Answer:

___

b $(9 \times 8) \times 4 + 6 - 1 =$

Answer:

___

c $3 \times (5 \times 7) + 11 - 8 =$

Answer:

___

d $6 + 9 - 5 \times (8 \times 3) =$

Answer:

___

e $9 - 7 + 6 \times 3 + (9 \times 6) =$

Answer:

___

f $6 + 9 \times 4 + (6 \times 7) - 21 =$

Answer:

___

Section A: Addition

Short-answer questions

Specific instructions to students

- This unit is designed to help you to improve your addition skills for basic operations.
- Read the questions below and answer all of them in the spaces provided.
- You may not use a calculator.
- You need to show all working.

QUESTION 1

A gardener measures four lengths of land for a new garden bed, which are 2 m, 1 m, 3 m and 5 m. How much length has been measured in total?

Answer:

QUESTION 2

The perimeter around some green areas needs to be cordoned off using rope. The sides of the areas measure 5 m, 8 m, 13 m and 15 m. How much rope is needed?

Answer:

QUESTION 3

A horticulture worker for a Parks and Gardens department needs to count stock at a warehouse. This includes 2170 cable ties that have been sorted by length, 368 pairs of gloves and 723 sets of safety glasses. How many items are in stock, in total?

Answer:

QUESTION 4

A horticultural worker who specialises in trees conducts a visual inspection for a pruning job. The number of trees that are inspected are 82 in the first area, 44 in the second area, 89 in the third area and 11 in the fourth area. How many trees have been inspected for pruning?

Answer:

QUESTION 5

Shutterstock.com/tommaso79

A horticulture assistant operates a whipper snipper and uses the following litres of fuel over four months: 32 litres, 47 litres, 57 litres and 59 litres. How many litres have been used in total?

Answer:

QUESTION 6

A gardener buys a small garden rake for $22, a 12 mm garden hose that is 15 m long for $16 and a 9-L plastic watering can for $9. How much money has the gardener spent?

Answer:

QUESTION 7

A horticulture assistant purchases some controlled-release fertilisers to be applied to the soil. The purchase consists of 1 kg for fruit and citrus trees and shrubs for $13, 4.5 kg all-purpose fertiliser for $39, 2 kg for native gardens for $23 and 9 kg all-purpose landscape fertiliser for $68. What is the total amount of money spent?

Answer:

QUESTION 8

An assistant gardener purchases a 190cc four-stroke ride-on petrol mower for $1589, four mower bar blades for $169 and two push lawn mowers for $209. How much money has been spent?

Answer:

_____

QUESTION 9

The lengths of instant turf that need to be laid for a client measure $16\,m^2$, $18\,m^2$, $8\,m^2$ and $11\,m^2$. How many square metres of instant turf is to be laid in total?

Answer:

_____

QUESTION 10

A particular soil at a housing estate requires nutrients to support tree and shrub growth. A gardener uses 178 litres of fertiliser on the first area, 188 litres on the second area and 93 litres on the third area. How many litres are used in total?

Answer:

_____

Section B: Subtraction

Short-answer questions

Specific instructions to students

- This section is designed to help you to improve your subtraction skills for basic operations.
- Read the questions below and answer all of them in the spaces provided.
- You may not use a calculator.
- You need to show all working.

QUESTION 1

An assistant gardener mixes 52 litres of pesticide at a ratio of $10\,mL$ per $1\,L$. If 12 litres are used in one week, 13 litres are used in the following week and 11 litres are used in the third week, how many litres are left?

Answer:

_____

QUESTION 2

Five hundred 30-litre bags of water-saving mulch are to be delivered to different landscaping worksites. If 250 bags are delivered first, then a further 125 bags, how many bags remain from the initial 500?

Answer:

_____

QUESTION 3

If 243 litres of pine bark mulch are used on one area and 159 litres are used on another area, how many more litres have been used on the first area compared to the second area?

Answer:

_____

QUESTION 4

If a gardener plants 12 nasturtium seeds from a packet of 90 seeds, how many are left?

Answer:

_____

QUESTION 5

A 25cc petrol blower vacuum mulcher is advertised for $230. The manager offers a discount of $27. How much does the customer pay?

Answer:

_____

9780170473385

QUESTION 6

A site manager orders 5000 pavers. Landscapers use 2756 pavers on various jobs. How many pavers remain?

Answer:

_____

QUESTION 7

According to a landscape plan, an area of land totals 96 m². If 44 m² is used for instant turf and 17 m² is used for gardens, how much land, in square metres, is left?

Answer:

_____

QUESTION 8

Alamy/Stephen Orsillo

A landscaper uses 69 200 mm 200 mm 40 mm masonry pavers on an area. If there were 105 pavers to begin with, how many remain?

Answer:

_____

QUESTION 9

The odometer of a landscaping work van has a reading of 56 089 km at the start of the year. At the end of the year, it reads 71 101 km. How many kilometres have been travelled during the year?

Answer:

_____

QUESTION 10

An assistant gardener uses 31 hardwood garden stakes (900 mm) to support plants in one area, 29 on plants in another area and 103 in the last area. If there were 250 stakes to begin with, how many are now left?

Answer:

_____

Section C: Multiplication

Short-answer questions

Specific instructions to students

- This section is designed to help you to improve your multiplication skills for basic operations.
- Read the following questions and answer all of them in the spaces provided.
- You may not use a calculator.
- You need to show all working.

QUESTION 1

A gardener charges $28 per hour. How much is earned for a 45-hour week?

Answer:

_____

QUESTION 2

If a horticulturalist finds 14 1-m steel garden posts in one box, how many are in 15 boxes?

Answer:

_____

QUESTION 3

A horticulture assistant uses 13 threaded mini spinners on one area of a garden. How many are needed for 18 similar areas?

Answer:

_____

QUESTION 4

A horticulturalist uses 12 metres of frost cloth on one area. How many metres are needed for 24 similar areas?

Answer:

_____

QUESTION 5

A gardener uses 5 m of weed-control mat for one area of the garden. How many metres of weed-control mat are needed for nine similar areas?

Answer:

_____

QUESTION 6

Sixteen litres of all-purpose potting mix is used to plant a shrub. How many litres are needed to plant 15 similar shrubs?

Answer:

_____

QUESTION 7

An assistant gardener uses 9 litres of two-stroke petrol mix in one day while using a petrol pruner. If the same amount is used over 12 days, how many litres are used in total?

Answer:

_____

QUESTION 8

If 673 litres of mulch is used per month by a council for landscaping parks and gardens, how many litres are used over a year?

Answer:

_____

QUESTION 9

If a horticulturalist plants four Drooping Sheoak trees each day, how many are planted during a 31-day month?

Answer:

_____

QUESTION 10

A horticulturalist plants 12 Silver Banksia trees over two weeks. How many trees are planted over 24 weeks, based on the same rate?

Answer:

_____

Section D: Division

Short-answer questions

Specific instructions to students

- This section is designed to help you to improve your division skills for basic operations.
- Read the questions below and answer all of them in the spaces provided.
- You may not use a calculator.
- You need to show all working.

QUESTION 1

An assistant gardener works a total of 24 hours over three days. How many hours are worked each day?

Answer:

_____

QUESTION 2

A landscaper earns $868 for working a five-day week. How much is earned per day?

Answer:

_____

9780170473385

QUESTION 3

Shutterstock.com/Stock Rocket

A client needs 140 seedlings planted in four separate areas of a housing development. How many seedlings are used in each area if they are planted evenly? Are there any seedlings left over?

Answer:

_____

QUESTION 4

A gardener needs to deliver 780 various plants to different locations over 12 days. On average, how many plants will be delivered per day?

Answer:

_____

QUESTION 5

Eighty-eight *Pittosporum angustifolium* need to be planted in four different inland areas around a country town. How many plants are allocated evenly to each area?

Answer:

_____

QUESTION 6

An assistant gardener lays 2975 pavers in seven different areas on a new housing estate. How many pavers are needed in each area if they are distributed evenly to the seven areas?

Answer:

_____

QUESTION 7

A worker at a landscaping company counts 2326 yellow post caps that have been stockpiled. If the post caps are stocked in lots of 100, how many lots are there? Are there any left over?

Answer:

_____

QUESTION 8

A landscaping business orders 408 bags of 20-litre compost. If the bags are put in six-bag lots, how many lots are there?

Answer:

_____

QUESTION 9

A horticulturalist orders 200 16-cm terracotta pots. They need to be divided up to be used at 12 different locations. How many will go to each location? Are there any left over?

Answer:

_____

QUESTION 10

A client of a major property development company orders 3890 m² of instant lawn to be used for 28 landholdings. How many square metres will be used at each landholding if the instant lawn is distributed evenly?

Answer:

_____

Section A: Addition

QUESTION 1

If a gardener buys four 220-litre compost bins for a total of $137.99 and a compost mixing tool for $22.70, how much is spent in total?

Answer:

_____

QUESTION 2

A horticulture company purchases a 10.8v li-ion cordless shrub shear for $39.95, a 1.8 kg fibreglass-handle axe for $29.95, a 240 mm tree lopper for $44.55 and a 750 mm bypass lopper for $19.45. How much money is spent?

Answer:

_____

QUESTION 3

A steel three-prong cultivator hoe costs $29.85, a 1 kg mini pick end costs $19.50 and a square-mouth shovel costs $15.65. What is the total cost?

Answer:

_____

QUESTION 4

A gardener purchases some 75 mm × 10 m black plastic garden edging for $26.98, some 150 mm × 6 m corrugated edging for $27.97, and some 600 mm × 5 m recycled garden edging for $28.99. What is the total cost?

Answer:

_____

QUESTION 5

An assistant gardener buys some cottage plants for a client, which include a blue *Limonium perezii* for $8.99, a 125-mm Patio Jewel Cinararias for $6.50, a 125-mm Double Flower Calibrachoa for $6.50 and two 140-mm Salvia Sierra for $25.99. What is the total cost?

Answer:

_____

QUESTION 6

If a gardener purchases four lots of reed fence screening, measuring 1.8 m × 3 m, for $65.80, a brushwood fence, measuring 1.8 m × 3 m, for $36.50, bamboo fence extensions, measuring 0.5 m × 2.4 m, for $22.70, and three lots of bark screen fencing for $89.90, how much has been spent for the client so far?

Answer:

_____

QUESTION 7

What is the total length of a 12-mm garden hose that measures 15.5 m and connects to another section that is 17.8 m?

Answer:

_____

QUESTION 8

A landscaper is asked to purchase items for a client who owns a winery. On the purchase list is a 38-inch 14.5hp gear drive petrol lawn tractor that costs $2420.50 and a 42-inch 17.5hp petrol ride-on lawn mower that costs $3790.50. What is the total cost for both?

Answer:

_____

 9780170473385

QUESTION 9

A horticulture worker needs to complete some tree maintenance. To complete the work, the worker needs to buy a 40-cm two-stroke bar petrol chainsaw for $206.50 and a 2.7-m 25.4cc petrol pole pruner for $330.95. How much is the worker charged in total?

Answer:

QUESTION 10

A gardener needs the following materials so that she can continue with the lawn maintenance for a client: a 5-litre fuel container that costs $9.35, a flexible spill-saver funnel that costs $5.98, a two-stroke fuel mixing bottle that costs $8.90, and a metal jerry can pourer that costs $14.98. How much will all four materials cost if you add the price together?

Answer:

Alamy/Tony Hobbs

Section B: Subtraction

Short-answer questions

Specific instructions to students

- This section is designed to help you to improve your subtraction skills when working with decimals.
- Read the questions below and answer all of them in the spaces provided.
- You may not use a calculator.
- You need to show all working.

QUESTION 1

A greenkeeper works on an 18-hole golf course and needs to cordon off an area that is a total of 12.5 metres long and contains two smaller areas. If rope is used to cordon off one smaller area measuring 388 mm and another smaller area measuring 295 mm, what is the length of edging that remains to be cordoned off?

Answer:

QUESTION 2

A groundskeeper is pruning trees but he needs the scissor lift to be lowered 225 cm from a height of 3.45 m. What is the new height?

Answer:

QUESTION 3

A lawn mowing company completes a large job on a commercial property and charges $789.20. A discount of $75.50 is given. How much is the final cost?

Answer:

QUESTION 4

A first-year horticulturalist works 38 hours in a week and earns $345.60. Petrol costs for the week come to $48.85. How much money is left?

Answer:

QUESTION 5

A scissor lift is used to reach a tree that has grown to a height of 3.60 m. The lift then needs to be lowered to a height of 2.95 m to work on the next section of the tree. How far has the scissor lift been lowered?

Answer:

_____

QUESTION 6

Two sections from the top of a 6-m palm tree need to be cut off. The two lengths measure 2.25 m and 2.8 m. How many metres are left from the original height of the palm tree?

Answer:

_____

QUESTION 7

A landscaping company has a spending balance of $4050.55. If two 190cc four-stroke ride-on petrol mowers are bought for $1550.50 each, how much money is left in the account?

Answer:

_____

QUESTION 8

A length of garden edging acts as a border for some landscape work. The edging measures 12.5 m. If a length of 9 m is cut from it, how much remains?

Answer:

_____

QUESTION 9

A mowing company has $5115.65 in their work account. The manager orders the following purchases: a 43cc two-stroke post hole digger for $349.15, a 2.3 m × 2.3 m × 1.9 m zinc garden shed for $395.00, and a 3.6 m × 3.0 m cut gable awning for $2517.95. How much is left in the account?

Answer:

_____

QUESTION 10

As part of a landscaping project, a city council orders 200 containers of seedlings for several different parks and gardens. If 50.5 are used on one project, 10.5 on another and 105.5 on two more different projects, how many containers are left?

Answer:

_____

Section C: Multiplication

Short-answer questions

Specific instructions to students

- This section is designed to help you to improve your multiplication skills when working with decimals.
- Read the questions below and answer all of them in the spaces provided.
- You may not use a calculator.
- You need to show all working.

QUESTION 1

If one 12 mm × 15 m garden hose costs $19.95, how much do five garden hoses cost?

Answer:

_____

QUESTION 2

If one leaf and grass rake costs $3.50, how much will 16 rakes cost?

Answer:

_____

QUESTION 3

iStockphoto/chrisroselli

Six fertiliser spreaders are purchased by a landscaping company at a cost of $74.50 each. What is the total cost for the six spreaders?

Answer:

_____

QUESTION 4

Six leaf scoops are bought for $8.65 each. What is the total cost?

Answer:

_____

QUESTION 5

A horticulturalist working in a nursery sells 12 kids' short handle garden trowels, which are on sale for $1.95 each. What is the total cost?

Answer:

_____

QUESTION 6

A horticulturalist working for the Parks and Gardens department of a council gets paid $34.50 per hour. If 38 hours are worked in one week, what is the gross wage (before tax)?

Answer:

_____

QUESTION 7

Assorted herbs are on special at a gardening centre for $2.55 each. If 25 are purchased, how much money has been spent?

Answer:

_____

QUESTION 8

A plant delivery van has a 52-litre tank. Fuel costs $1.35 per litre. How much does it cost to fill the tank?

Answer:

_____

QUESTION 9

A landscaper lays 3400 pavers. Each paver costs $2.35. What is the total cost for the pavers?

Answer:

_____

QUESTION 10

A farmhand earns $160.65 per day. What is the gross weekly wage (before tax) for five days of work?

Answer:

_____

Section D: Division

Short-answer questions

Specific instructions to students

- This section is designed to help you to improve your division skills when working with decimals.
- Read the questions below and answer all of them in the spaces provided.
- You may not use a calculator.
- You need to show all working.

QUESTION 1

A landscaper uses 28.5 m² of Santa Ana couch grass on six separate equal-sized areas in a new housing development. How much is equally allocated for each area?

Answer:

_____

QUESTION 2

Five 220-litre compost bins are purchased for $990.50. How much does each compost bin cost?

Answer:

_____

QUESTION 3

A landscaper has finished working on a housing estate and charges $3732.70 for the work. It took 50 hours to complete the work, so what is the rate per hour, inclusive of labour and materials?

Answer:

QUESTION 4

A casual maintenance worker gets paid $600.85 for 27 hours of work. What is the hourly rate?

Answer:

QUESTION 5

A mowing company charges $3368 for seven major lawn mowing contracts for seven commercial properties. How much is each contract worth?

Answer:

QUESTION 6

A gardener charges a total of $889.95 for nine separate jobs, which include tree pruning, mowing and edge trimming. On average, how much is charged for each job?

Answer:

QUESTION 7

Over a period of time, a 30cc two-stroke petrol line trimmer uses 36 spools of line at a total cost of $225.80. How much does each spool cost?

Answer:

QUESTION 8

Shutterstock.com/sematadesign

A casual nursery worker works for five days and gets paid $840. How much is he paid per day (before tax)?

Answer:

QUESTION 9

A gardener buys 15 mixed confetti petunia flower seed packets for a total of $62.25. How much does each packet cost?

Answer:

QUESTION 10

Ten 10-kg bags of granulated soil wetter are purchased for $185.20. What is the cost for one bag?

Answer:

9780170473385

Unit 7: Fractions

Section A: Addition

QUESTION 1

$\frac{1}{2} + \frac{4}{5} =$

Answer:

_____

QUESTION 2

$2\frac{2}{4} + 1\frac{2}{3} =$

Answer:

_____

QUESTION 3

A gardener adds $\frac{1}{3}$ of a bag of manure to another bag of manure that is already $\frac{1}{4}$ full. How much manure is there in the bag, as a fraction?

Answer:

_____

QUESTION 4

A gardener uses $\frac{1}{2}$ of a bag of all-purpose natural mulch in one area of the garden and $\frac{1}{3}$ of a bag of pine bark mulch in a different area. How much mulch has been added to both areas, as a fraction?

Answer:

_____

QUESTION 5

A groundskeeper adds 1 and $\frac{2}{3}$ bags of pea straw mulch around one area of a garden and 1 and $\frac{1}{4}$ bags of lucerne mulch in another area. What is the total amount of mulch added to the two areas, as a fraction?

Answer:

_____

Section B: Subtraction

QUESTION 1

$\frac{2}{3} - \frac{1}{4} =$

Answer:

QUESTION 2

$2\frac{2}{3} - 1\frac{1}{4} =$

Answer:

QUESTION 3

A full bag of water-saving mulch is distributed around a flower garden. If $\frac{1}{6}$ of the mulch from the bag is used on a small area, then a further $\frac{1}{4}$ is distributed over another area, how much remains in the bag, as a fraction?

Answer:

_____

QUESTION 4

A bag of sugar cane mulch is $\frac{3}{4}$ full. If $\frac{1}{8}$ is used on a landscaped area, how much is left, as a fraction?

Answer:

_____

QUESTION 5

A gardener has 2 and $\frac{1}{2}$ bags of all-purpose potting mix. If 1 and $\frac{1}{3}$ bags are used for potting plants, how much is left, as a fraction?

Answer:

_____

Section C: Multiplication

Short-answer questions

Specific instructions to students

- This section is designed to help you to improve your multiplication skills when working with fractions.
- Read the questions below and answer all of them in the spaces provided.
- You may not use a calculator.
- You need to show all working.

QUESTION 1

$\frac{2}{4} \times \frac{2}{3} =$

Answer:

_____

QUESTION 2

$2\frac{2}{3} \times 1\frac{1}{2} =$

Answer:

_____

QUESTION 3

Fifteen halved wine barrels are filled with potting mix to halfway. How many full wine barrels would this make?

Answer:

_____

Shutterstock.com/Chiyacat

9780170473385

QUESTION 4

There are 8 and $\frac{1}{2}$ bags of potting mix that can be used for roses, gardenias, azaleas and camellias. If each bag weighs 25 litres, how many litres are there in total, as a fraction?

Answer:

QUESTION 5

An apprentice horticulturalist has 2 and $\frac{1}{2}$ bags of 25-litre native potting and planting mix that needs to be used for native shrubs. How many litres is there in total, as a fraction?

Answer:

Section D: Division

Short-answer questions

Specific instructions to students

- This section is designed to help you to improve your division skills when working with fractions.
- Read the questions below and answer all of them in the spaces provided.
- You may not use a calculator.
- You need to show all working.

QUESTION 1

$\frac{2}{3} \div \frac{1}{4} =$

Answer:

QUESTION 2

$2\frac{3}{4} \div 1\frac{1}{3} =$

Answer:

QUESTION 3

A landscaper works 37 and $\frac{1}{2}$ hours over five days. How many hours per day has she worked, as a fraction?

Answer:

QUESTION 4

If a gardener has 2 and $\frac{1}{2}$ 25-litre bags of premium potting mix that needs to be used on three different jobs, what fraction is to be used on each job?

Answer:

QUESTION 5

A gardener at a nursery needs to distribute 25 litres of tomato and vegetable growing mix into seven 28-cm plastic self-watering pots. What fraction of mix will go into each pot?

Answer:

Unit 8: Percentages

Short-answer questions

Specific instructions to students

- In this unit, you will be able to practise and improve your skills in working out percentages.
- Read the questions below and answer all of them in the spaces provided.
- You may not use a calculator.
- You need to show all working.

> 10% rule: move the decimal one place to the left to get 10%.

EXAMPLE

10% of $45.00 is $4.50.

QUESTION 1

A city council pays $5220.00 for an Occupation Health and Safety course for a large number of new employees. The company conducting the course gives a discount of 10%.

a How much is the discount worth?

Answer:

b What is the final cost?

Answer:

QUESTION 2

A fall protection kit that is required by a tree lopper using a scissor lift costs $249.00. A 10% discount is given at a sale. What is the final cost after 10% is taken off?

Answer:

QUESTION 3

Six pairs of all-terrain gel knee pads are bought for $698.00. If the company gets a 10% trade discount, how much will the six pairs of gel knee pads cost?

Answer:

QUESTION 4

A pair of professional safety goggles is bought for $24.60. A 5% discount is given.

a How much is the discount worth?

Answer:

b What is the final price? (Hint: Find 10%, halve it and then subtract it from the overall price.)

Answer:

QUESTION 5

A pair of gardening gloves costs $20, a heavy-duty support belt costs $69 and two XL yellow hi-vis safety vests cost $10.50.

a How much is the total?

Answer:

b How much is paid after a 10% discount?

Answer:

QUESTION 6

A gardener purchases a 7-piece safety kit for $19.99, a pair of safety glasses for $9.99, a chainsaw safety kit for $89.99, a pair of safety gloves for $6.99 and a 15-m extension lead for $14.99.

a What is the total?

Answer:

9780170473385

b What is the final cost after a 10% discount?

Answer:

_____

QUESTION 7

A hardware store offers 20% off the price of 430-mm round grower pots. The pots normally cost $9 each before the discount. How much will they cost after the discount?

Answer:

_____

QUESTION 8

As part of a hardware and garden store's marketing campaign, 12-mm brass jet spray guns are discounted by 15%. If the regular retail price is $25.99 each, what is the discounted price?

Answer:

_____

QUESTION 9

Shutterstock.com/yanami

The regular retail price of a 19 mm × 50 m black poly drip irrigation tube is $29.90. The store has a 20% sale. How much will it cost during the sale?

Answer:

_____

QUESTION 10

A universal poly pipe cutter normally costs $9.98. How much does it cost after the store takes off 30% during an end-of-financial-year sale?

Answer:

_____

Unit 9: Measurement Conversions

QUESTION 1

How many millimetres are there in 1 cm?

Answer:

QUESTION 2

How many millimetres are there in 1 m?

Answer:

QUESTION 3

How many centimetres are there in 1 m?

Answer:

QUESTION 4

The length of one side of a garden is 2550 mm. What is the length in metres?

Answer:

QUESTION 5

The length of a garden edging is 3650 mm. How many metres is this?

Answer:

QUESTION 6

The bunting used to surround and protect a garden that is being repaired measures 2.6 m. How many millimetres is this?

Answer:

QUESTION 7

A piece of garden hose that measures 2850 mm is joined to another piece of hose that measures 3250 mm. What is the total length of the garden hose, in metres?

Answer:

QUESTION 8

A landscaper has three separate sections of Fescue instant lawn to use on different jobs. They measure 2.45 m², 3.15 m² and 1.85 m². What is the total of instant lawn used, in squared millimetres?

Answer:

QUESTION 9

A garden bed has three sides that require edging. The sides measure 2580 mm, 1325 mm and 2400 mm. How long is the required edging, in metres?

Answer:

QUESTION 10

A horticulturalist reads from a landscape plan that includes a rectangular garden with the dimensions of 2850 mm, 2350 mm, 2850 mm and 2350 mm. What is the total perimeter of the garden, in metres?

Answer:

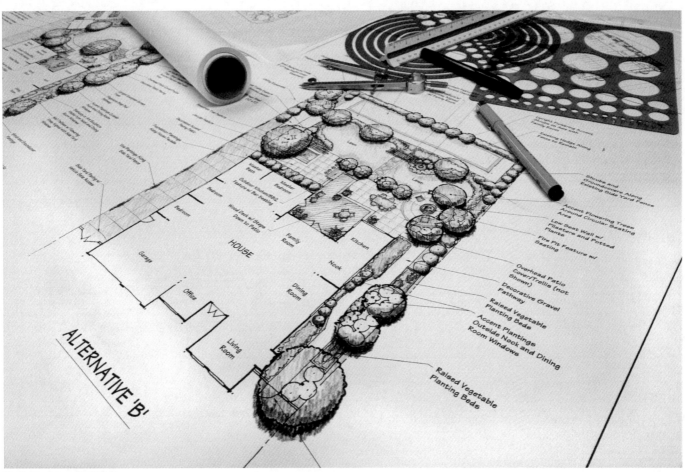

Shutterstock.com/Scott E. Feuer

Section A: Area

> Area = length × breadth and is given in square units
>
> $= l \times b$

QUESTION 1

The dimensions of a garden bed are $3\,m \times 2.8\,m$ wide. What is the total area?

Answer:

_____

QUESTION 2

If a flower bed measures $2.2\,m \times 1.3\,m$, what is the total area?

Answer:

_____

QUESTION 3

An area designated for instant lawn measures $3.5\,m^2 \times 3.65\,m^2$. What is the total area?

Answer:

_____

QUESTION 4

An area for growing vegetables measures $2.1\,m \times 0.8\,m$. What is the total area?

Answer:

_____

QUESTION 5

An area set aside for growing bulbs in pots measures $3.3\,m \times 3.5\,m$. What is the total area?

Answer:

_____

QUESTION 6

The floor of a garden shed measures $3.55\,m \times 3.28\,m$. What is the total area?

Answer:

_____

QUESTION 7

The measurement of an area where fruit trees will be planted is $4.5\,m \times 2.5\,m$. What is the total area?

Answer:

_____

QUESTION 8

A lettuce garden is $3.5\,m \times 3.2\,m$. What is the total area?

Answer:

_____

QUESTION 9

A timber deck measures $3.2\,m$ wide $\times 8.6\,m$ long. What is the deck area?

Answer:

_____

QUESTION 10

The area for a pond is 2.9 m long × 2.6 m wide. What is the total area?

Answer:

123rf/David Seaford

Section B: Perimeter

Perimeter is the length of all sides added together.

> Perimeter = length + breadth + length + breadth

The unit of measurement is either in metres, centimetres or millimetres.

QUESTION 1

Dwarf lilly pillys are being planted around the edge of a lawn area. Calculate the perimeter of a lawn that is 13 m long × 9 m wide before planting the hedges.

Answer:

QUESTION 2

A paling fence needs to be constructed around the perimeter of an area that will house compost bins. The dimensions are 3.2 m × 2.6 m. What is the perimeter?

Answer:

QUESTION 3

A pond is being planned for a backyard garden area that measures 4.8 m × 3.8 m. The client would like a fence constructed around the pond. What is the measurement of the perimeter of the fenced area?

Answer:

QUESTION 4

A pebbled garden bed measures 6.5 m × 2.7 m. Edging needs to be placed around the perimeter. What is the perimeter measurement for the edging?

Answer:

QUESTION 5

Pavers are being laid around the perimeter of a garden that measures 3.4 m × 3.7 m. What is the length of the perimeter?

Answer:

QUESTION 6

A client wants a timber deck that measures 2.85 m × 2.35 m directly outside their back door. Around the deck, the client has requested hedges be planted. What is the perimeter of the deck?

Answer:

_____

QUESTION 7

A paved area is 4.65 m × 3.85 m and the client wants a garden bed around the perimeter. What length does the perimeter measure?

Answer:

_____

QUESTION 8

A pergola area has the dimensions of 3.75 m × 3.95 m. What is the perimeter?

Answer:

_____

QUESTION 9

The building plan of a garage includes floor measurements of 5.55 m × 4.65 m. What is the perimeter?

Answer:

_____

QUESTION 10

A paved area for a spa measures 2.75 m × 2.95 m. What is the total perimeter?

Answer:

_____

Section C: Volume of a rectangle

Short-answer questions

Specific instructions to students

- This section is designed to help you to improve your skills and to increase your speed in measuring the volume of a rectangle.
- Read the questions below and answer all of them in the spaces provided.
- You may not use a calculator.
- You need to show all working.

> Volume = length × width × height and is given in cubic units
>
> $= l \times \omega \times h$

QUESTION 1

A trailer is being used to transport soil for the top of a garden that measures 3 m × 2 m × 0.1 m. How many cubic metres of soil are needed?

Answer:

_____

QUESTION 2

An area is being prepared for instant turf to be laid. The area measures 8 m × 5 m and to a depth of 0.1 m. How many cubic metres of turf are needed?

Answer:

_____

9780170473385

QUESTION 3

A landscaper wants to spread mulch over an area that measures 19 m × 13 m and to a thickness of 0.075 m. How many cubic metres of mulch are needed?

Answer:

_____

QUESTION 4

Topsoil with a sand-base mix is being spread to a depth of 150 mm, using a lawn-level spreader bar, across a lawn after it has been mowed. The lawn is 12.2 m × 1.8 m. How many cubic metres of topsoil are needed?

Answer:

_____

QUESTION 5

Shutterstock.com/Stacey Barnett

Play-grade bark is used to cover a play area in a park that measures 16 m × 15 m × 300 mm. How many cubic metres of bark are required?

Answer:

_____

QUESTION 6

Soil improver is used on heavy clay soil in an area that measures 4.2 m × 4.2 m × 75 mm. How many cubic metres of soil are needed?

Answer:

_____

QUESTION 7

Lawn topdressing needs to be spread in spring and autumn. The area of lawn is 30 m long × 25 m wide and needs soil improver to a depth of 3 mm. How many cubic metres of topdressing are needed?

Answer:

_____

QUESTION 8

A lawn requires a topdressing to level it out and fill some holes and low spots. The lawn is mowed and then a clean sandy loam soil is applied. The lawn area dimensions are 6.5 m × 9.5 m to a depth of 0.01 m. How much sandy loam is needed, in cubic metres?

Answer:

_____

QUESTION 9

The area of a local playground measures 13.5 m wide × 13.6 m. Play-grade bark is used to cover the top of the area to a depth of 300 mm. How many cubic metres of bark are needed?

Answer:

_____

QUESTION 10

Topsoil is added before laying turf in an area of a bowling club. The dimensions are 33.8 m × 22.8 m × 150 mm. How many cubic metres of topsoil are required?

Answer:

_____

Section D: Volume of a circle

Short-answer questions

Specific instructions to students

- This section is designed to help you to improve your skills and to increase your speed in measuring the volume of a circle.
- Read the questions below and answer all of them in the spaces provided.
- You may not use a calculator.
- You need to show all working.

> Volume = length × width × height and is given in cubic units

Hint: For the surface area of a circle use: π (pi = 3.14) × radius squared (work out radius squared first and then times by π) then × by height/depth. You might like to draw a diagram for each question to help you solve the problem!

QUESTION 1

A circular pond has a radius of 2 m across and is 0.5 m deep. What is the volume of water in the pond, in cubic metres?

Answer:

QUESTION 2

A water feature consists of two differently sized round ponds that are joined. The first pond has a radius of 2 m and is 0.5 m deep. The second pond has a radius of 3 m and is also 0.5 m deep. What is the total volume of the water feature, in cubic metres?

Answer:

QUESTION 3

A Chinese water feature has three circular ponds that are joined together and share the water. Each circle has a different radius. The first circle is 1 m, the second circle is 2 m and the third circle is 3 m. The depth of the water is 0.3 m. What volume of water is needed to fill the whole feature, in cubic metres?

Answer:

QUESTION 4

A planting bed that is in the shape of a semi-circle has a diameter of 4 m. Soil is added to it to a depth of 0.3 m. How much soil is needed, in cubic metres?

Answer:

QUESTION 5

Two separate garden beds are both semi-circular and each has a diameter of 2.4 m. If soil is added to a depth of 0.2 m, how much is needed for both garden beds, in cubic metres?

Answer:

QUESTION 6

Six circular areas that have a radius of 2.2 m are being prepared for planting shrubs. Soil has to be added to a depth of 0.5 m in each area.

a How much soil is needed for each area, in cubic metres?

Answer:

b How much soil is needed in total for all six areas?

Answer:

9780170473385

QUESTION 7

An area is being prepared for landscaping. It consists of two circular areas and one semi-circular area. The circular areas are the same size and both have a diameter of 3.6 m. The semi-circular area has a radius of 1.6 m. The areas are being excavated to a depth of 0.3 m. How much compacted soil will be excavated from the area, in cubic metres?

Answer:

QUESTION 8

Two large circular areas in a park are being used for new garden beds. Each measures 12.6 m in diameter. If the material being excavated is 0.5 m deep, how many cubic metres will be removed?

Answer:

QUESTION 9

A client wants seven circular paved steps as part of their garden landscape. Each circular step has a diameter of 3 m. Each one needs to have paving sand added to a depth of 0.25 m.

a   How many cubic metres of paving sand is needed for each step?

Answer:

b   How many cubic metres of paving sand is needed for all seven steps?

Answer:

QUESTION 10

A circular lawn needs topdressing. The lawn measures 7.8 m in diameter and the depth of the topdressing will be 0.1 m. How much topdressing is needed, in cubic metres?

Answer:

Unit 11: Time, Motion and Money

Short-answer questions

Specific instructions to students

- This unit is designed to help you to calculate how much a job is worth and how long you need to complete the job.
- Read the questions below and answer all of them in the spaces provided.
- You may not use a calculator.
- You need to show all working.

QUESTION 1

Shutterstock.com/michaeljung

A first-year horticulturalist working at a nursery earns $18 per hour and works a 38-hour week. How much is earned per year? (Remember: there are 52 weeks in a year.)

Answer:

_____

QUESTION 2

A nursery manager starts work at 7.00 a.m. and stops for a break at 9.30 a.m. for 20 minutes. Lunch starts at 1.15 p.m. and is for 30 minutes. The nursery manager then works until 4 p.m. How many hours have been worked, including breaks?

Answer:

_____

QUESTION 3

An experienced landscaper earns $31.00 an hour and works a 38-hour week. How much is her weekly gross earnings (before tax)?

Answer:

_____

QUESTION 4

Over five weeks, a self-employed landscape gardener completes five jobs. After completing the work, he issues invoices for $465.80, $2490.50, $556.20, $1560.70 and $990.60. What is the total to be paid for all of the completed jobs?

Answer:

_____

QUESTION 5

A gardener takes 34 minutes to unload bags of compost, mulch and sand from the work van. It takes eight minutes to prepare the materials for spreading over a lawn, four minutes to carry the bags to the worksite and 27 minutes to complete the work. How much time has been taken on this job? (Give your answer in hours and minutes.)

Answer:

_____

QUESTION 6

A landscaper takes four and a half hours to weed invasive species, prune and fertilise fruit trees and water the grounds. If the landscaping company charges a rate of $28.60 an hour, what is the bill for this work?

Answer:

_____

QUESTION 7

A landscape labourer takes 7.5 hours to plant and renovate grassed areas. If the rate of pay is $14.80 per hour, what is the total bill?

Answer:

_____

 9780170473385

QUESTION 8

A landscaper spends 116 hours to plant, transport and prune trees and shrubs, and to build some landscape features. If he works 7.5-hour days, how many days does it take to complete the job?

Answer:

_____

QUESTION 9

A landscape supervisor begins work at 7.00 a.m. and works until 3.30 p.m. She takes a morning break for 20 minutes, a lunch break for 60 minutes and an afternoon break for 20 minutes.

a   How much time has she spent on breaks?

Answer:

_____

b   How much time has she spent working?

Answer:

_____

Shutterstock.com/Slasha

QUESTION 10

The cost of a landscape project is $860.00. The landscape manager spends 24 hours designing landscape structures and features as well as meeting and negotiating with clients. How much is the rate of pay per hour?

Answer:

_____

Unit 12: Squaring Numbers

Section A: Introducing square numbers

Short-answer questions

Specific instructions to students

- This section is designed to help you to improve your skills and to increase your speed in squaring numbers.
- Read the questions below and answer all of them in the spaces provided.
- You may not use a calculator.
- You need to show all working.

Any number squared is multiplied by itself.

EXAMPLE

4 squared $= 4^2 = 4 \times 4 = 16$

QUESTION 1

$6^2 =$

Answer:

_____

QUESTION 2

$8^2 =$

Answer:

_____

QUESTION 3

$12^2 =$

Answer:

_____

QUESTION 4

$3^2 =$

Answer:

_____

QUESTION 5

$7^2 =$

Answer:

_____

QUESTION 6

$11^2 =$

Answer:

_____

QUESTION 7

$10^2 =$

Answer:

_____

QUESTION 8

$9^2 =$

Answer:

_____

QUESTION 9

$2^2 =$

Answer:

_____

QUESTION 10

$4^2 =$

Answer:

_____

Section B: Applying square numbers to the trade

QUESTION 1

An area is put aside for a banksia, which is a native plant and requires less watering. The area measures 2.8 m × 2.8 m. What is the total area, in square metres?

Answer:

QUESTION 2

A golden wattle (*Acacia pycnantha*) is planted in an area that is 5.2 m × 5.2 m. What is the total area, in square metres?

Answer:

QUESTION 3

The dimensions for an area to plant a swamp saltbush (*Atriplex amnicola)* are 4.6 m × 4.6 m. What is the total area, in square metres?

Answer:

QUESTION 4

A White Cypress-pine (*Callitris columellaris*) is planted in an area that measures 15 m × 15 m. How much area is this, in square metres?

Answer:

QUESTION 5

A Zamia fern (*Bowenia spectabilis*) needs to be planted in a client's yard, in an area that measures 1.8 m × 1.8 m. A pond also needs to be constructed in the same yard, in an area that has the dimensions of 6.5 m × 6.5 m. The rest of the yard is to be grassed. If the yard measures 13.4 m × 13.4 m, how much grassed area is there?

Answer:

QUESTION 6

A mountain grevillea (*Grevillea alpina*) is planted in a plot that measures 2.45 m × 2.45 m. What is the total area, in square metres?

Answer:

QUESTION 7

Shutterstock.com/Ingrid Balabanova

A client wants instant turf laid as their front lawn. The area measures 6.8 m × 6.8 m.

a   How many square metres of instant turf is needed?

Answer:

b What is the total cost if the instant lawn costs $8.50 per square metre?

Answer:

_____

QUESTION 8

New pavers are laid in an area that measures 4.5 m × 4.5 m. There are 36 pavers laid per square metre, which includes an allowance for any damaged pavers. How many pavers are needed?

Answer:

_____

QUESTION 9

Three garden beds measure 6 m × 3 m each, and have silverbush (*Convolvulus cneorum*) planted in them. The planting density is three plants per square metre.

a How many plants are needed for each garden bed?

Answer:

_____

b How many plants are needed for the three garden beds?

Answer:

_____

c If each plant is $9.50, what will be the total cost for the plants?

Answer:

_____

QUESTION 10

Two garden beds measure 15 m × 4 m each, and have a 140 mm groundcover planted in them. The planting density is three plants per square metre.

a How many plants are needed for each garden bed?

Answer:

_____

b How many plants are needed for the two garden beds?

Answer:

_____

c If each groundcover plant is $10.35, what will be the total cost for the plants?

Answer:

_____

9780170473385

Unit 13: Ratios

Section A: Introducing ratios

Short-answer questions

Specific instructions to students

- This section is designed to help you to improve your skills and to increase your speed in calculating and simplifying ratios.
- Read the questions below and answer all of them in the spaces provided.
- You may not use a calculator.
- You need to show all working.
- Reduce the ratios to the simplest or lowest form.

QUESTION 1

To make a two-stroke mix for a weed trimmer, a gardener needs to use a ratio of 25 : 1 fuel to oil mix. How much oil is added to 1 L of fuel?

Answer:

_____

QUESTION 2

To make a two-stroke mix for a lawn mower, a gardener needs to use a ratio of 25 : 1 fuel to oil mix. How much oil is added to 5 L of fuel?

Answer:

_____

QUESTION 3

To make a two-stroke mix for a tree pruner, a gardener needs to use a ratio of 25 : 1 fuel to oil mix. How much oil is added to 20 L of fuel?

Answer:

_____

QUESTION 4

An instruction manual for a chainsaw suggests that a 50 : 1 fuel to oil ratio should be used. How much oil is needed to be mixed to 1 L of fuel?

Answer:

_____

QUESTION 5

A chainsaw needs a two-stroke fuel in the ratio of 50 : 1 fuel to oil. How much oil needs to be mixed to 5 L of fuel?

Answer:

_____

QUESTION 6

An instruction manual for a chainsaw suggests that a 50 : 1 fuel to oil ratio should be used. How much oil needs to be mixed to 20 L of fuel?

Answer:

_____

QUESTION 7

A brushcutter needs a two-stroke fuel mix in the ratio of 25 : 1 fuel to oil. If 3 L of fuel is provided, how much oil is added?

Answer:

_____

QUESTION 8

A 25-L container is full of petrol. Oil needs to be mixed with it to make a two-stroke mix so that it can be poured into a mower. If you use the ratio of 25 : 1 fuel to oil mix, how much oil should be added?

Answer:

_____

QUESTION 9

A 10-L fuel container is full of unleaded petrol. How much oil is added to the petrol if a 25 : 1 fuel to oil two-stroke ratio is required?

Answer:

QUESTION 10

A 30cc garden yard petrol backpack leaf blower runs on a two-stroke mix. If there are 500 millilitres of fuel, how much oil is added at a ratio of 25 : 1 fuel to oil?

Answer:

iStockphoto/scottyspics

9780170473385

Unit 14: Applying Maths to the Horticulture Trade

Section A: Wages

Short-answer questions

Specific instructions to students

- This section is designed to help you to improve your Maths skills in the horticulture trade.
- Read the questions below and answer all of them in the spaces provided.
- You may not use a calculator.
- You need to show all working.
- Reduce the ratios to the simplest or lowest form.

QUESTION 1

A gardener gets paid $22.50 per hour and works a 38-hour week. How much is earned for the working week, before tax?

Answer:

_____

QUESTION 2

A landscape gardener earns $26.50 per hour and works for 76 hours over a fortnight. How much is earned, before tax?

Answer:

_____

QUESTION 3

A junior nursery worker gets paid $18.75 per hour and works for 38 hours per week. How much is earned per week, before tax?

Answer:

_____

QUESTION 4

A horticulturalist earns $28.50 an hour, works 38 hours per week and gets paid fortnightly. How much is earned, before tax?

Answer:

_____

QUESTION 5

A nursery manager gets paid $25.75 per hour, works 38 hours per week and gets paid weekly. After being paid, the nursery manager spends $35.50 on petrol, $47.50 on food and $62.75 on entertainment. How much is left over?

Answer:

_____

QUESTION 6

A farmer earns $52 193 for the year. How much is the weekly income, before tax?

Answer:

_____

QUESTION 7

A farmhand earns $19.54 per hour and works a 45-hour week. How much is earned, before tax?

Answer:

_____

QUESTION 8

A grounds maintenance worker earns $50 401 per year. How much is the weekly wage, before tax?

Answer:

_____

QUESTION 9

A landscape labourer gets paid $764.56 for a week's work. The landscape labourer spends $86 on tools, $49 on personal protective equipment (PPE) and $18 on medical insurance. How much is left?

Answer:

QUESTION 10

A groundskeeper gets paid $1697.84 for a fortnight's work. Her fortnightly expenses include $45.50 for clothes, $42.90 for food and $180.50 for car registration. How much is left after all the expenses?

Answer:

Section B: Flow rates and chemicals

Short-answer questions

Specific instructions to students

- This section is designed to help you to improve your Maths skills in the horticulture trade.
- Read the questions below and answer all of them in the spaces provided.
- You may not use a calculator.
- You need to show all working.
- Reduce the ratios to the simplest or lowest form.

QUESTION 1

The tank on a backpack sprayer holds 20 L of liquid. If the sprayer has a flow rate of 1.25 litres per minute, approximately how long will it take for the sprayer to run out?

Answer:

QUESTION 2

The tank on a backpack sprayer holds 20 L of liquid. If the sprayer has a flow rate of 1.75 litres per minute, approximately how long will it take for the sprayer to run out?

Answer:

QUESTION 3

There are 18 holes on a golf course. Each green needs to be sprayed, to kill off any weeds. If it takes an average of 12 minutes to spray each green, how long will it take to spray all 18 greens?

Answer:

QUESTION 4

A gardener needs to rid their garden of scale insects and mealybugs. A 10-L sprayer is filled with the oil preparation. The sprayer rate is 1.5 litres per minute. How long before the sprayer runs out?

Answer:

QUESTION 5

Aphids and caterpillars have become a problem in a garden and they need to be controlled. A natural solution of soap flakes and water is made up and added to a 20-L backpack sprayer. The spray rate is 2.5 litres per minute. How long will the solution last?

Answer:

Shutterstock.com/Windyboy

9780170473385

QUESTION 6

A 450-mL insecticide sprayer that contains pyrethrum is used in a garden to control insects that are on plants, vegetables and fruit trees. If a 1-L container of spray costs $11.28, how much will five spray bottles cost?

Answer:

QUESTION 7

A gardener uses a 500-g can of tomato and vegetable dust to protect specific plants. If one can costs $10.65, how much will seven cans cost?

Answer:

QUESTION 8

A landscaper purchases a 5-L container of eco-oil to kill off insects in the garden. The cost of the container is $39.95. What is the cost per litre?

Answer:

QUESTION 9

A nursery worker purchases some lime sulphur concentrate to spray fruit trees and roses during winter, to control mites and leaf curl. A 500-mL spray bottle costs $13.69. How much will three bottles cost?

Answer:

QUESTION 10

Four spray bottles of 500-g triforine fungicide are bought to control systemic fungus in rose bushes. The total cost is $102.60. How much is each bottle?

Answer:

Section C: Spray time

Short-answer questions

Specific instructions to students

- This section is designed to help you to improve your Maths skills in the horticulture trade.
- Read the questions below and answer all of them in the spaces provided.
- You may not use a calculator.
- You need to show all working.
- Reduce the ratios to the simplest or lowest form.

QUESTION 1

An assistant gardener wants to spray a citrus crop that has been affected by citrus leafminer (*Phyllocnistis citrella*) with a ground application rate of 10 mL of insecticide per 100 L of water. The application needs to be carried out every 21 days. If a spraying backpack holds 20 L, how much insecticide needs to be added to the water?

Answer:

QUESTION 2

A nursery worker wants to spray green beans that have native budworm (*Helicoverpa punctigera*) in them. The worker decides to use an application rate of 200 mL of insecticide per 500 L of water. The spray needs to be applied at flowering and a higher rate needs to be used if the larvae are larger than 1 cm. If a spraying backpack holds 20 L, how much insecticide needs to be added to the water?

Answer:

QUESTION 3

A gardener wants to spray a cabbage garden that has been infected by cabbage moth (*Plutella xylostella*). The ground application rate is 100 mL of insecticide per 1000 L of water. If a spraying backpack holds 10 L, how much insecticide needs to be added to the water?

Answer:

Shutterstock.com/shama65

QUESTION 4

A potato farmer has a problem with potato moth (*Phthorimaea operculella*) affecting his crops. The farmer decides to use an application rate of 200 mL of insecticide per 1500 L of water. If the spraying backpack holds 20 L, how much insecticide needs to be added to the water?

Answer:

QUESTION 5

Tomato grub (*Helicoverpa armigera*) is infecting a tomato grower's plants. The grower decides to use an application rate of 200 mL of insecticide per 250 L of water. If the spraying backpack holds 20 L, how much insecticide needs to be added to the water?

Answer:

QUESTION 6

Nursery flowers and other ornamental plants have been infected by light brown apple moth (*Epiphyas postvittana*). A nursery worker decides to use an application rate of 150 mL of insecticide per 1000 L of water. If the spraying backpack holds 16 L, how much insecticide needs to be added to the water?

Answer:

QUESTION 7

Brussels sprouts and broccoli plants have been infected by cabbage white butterfly (*Pieris rapae*) in a vegetable patch. The gardener decides to use an application rate of 100 mL of insecticide per 600 L of water. The spraying backpack holds 15 L. How much insecticide needs to be added to the water?

Answer:

QUESTION 8

A different vegetable garden that grows brussels sprouts and broccoli plants has also been infected by cabbage white butterfly. The gardener decides to use an application rate of 100 mL of insecticide per 800 L of water. The spraying backpack holds 10 L. How much insecticide needs to be added to the water?

Answer:

QUESTION 9

An assistant garden worker grows cauliflowers, but they have been infected by cabbage moth (*Plutella xylostella*). The assistant decides that an application of 100 mL of insecticide in 800 L of water will be used. The assistant has a spray bottle that only holds 1 L. How much insecticide is to be added to the spray bottle?

Answer:

QUESTION 10

A crop of sweet corn has been infected by *Helicoverpa armigera*. An application of 200 mL of insecticide to 450 L of water is required. The sprayer holds 1.5 L. How much insecticide needs to be added to the sprayer?

Answer:

9780170473385

Section D: Planning a garden landscape

EXAMPLE

If a scale on a landscape plan is given as 1:100, this means that 1 cm on the plan is equivalent to 100 cm (or 1 m) in the actual landscape.

QUESTION 1

A landscape plan has existing landscape features such as a house, a driveway and a garage that need to be drawn on the preliminary design. The fence line will have flowering trees, medium flowering shrubs, a perennial bed and a pond next to it. The scale on the plan is 1:100.

a If the fence measures 18 cm on the plan, how many metres will the fence be?

Answer:

b If the pond measures 4 cm × 3 cm on the plan, how many square metres will the pond be?

Answer:

QUESTION 2

On the same landscape plan, a shade tree is drawn with a 4.5 cm diameter. How many metres will this allow for the tree?

Answer:

QUESTION 3

A circular annual bed measures 3.4 cm in diameter on the same plan. What is the surface area of the annual bed?

Answer:

QUESTION 4

A perennial bed measures 2.5 cm × 4.5 cm on the same landscape plan. What is the rectangular surface area, in metres?

Answer:

QUESTION 5

A paved area that measures 8.5 cm × 2.5 cm is drawn on the plan.

a What is the total area, in square metres?

Answer:

b If there are 36 pavers per square metre, how many pavers are needed?

Answer:

QUESTION 6

An area is being prepared for instant lawn. On the plan, the area measures 9.3 cm × 4.7 cm.

a What is the total area, in square metres?

Answer:

b If instant lawn costs $5.24 per 0.5 m², how much will it cost to lay instant lawn on this area?

Answer:

QUESTION 7

A garden bed measures 12.8 cm × 1.2 cm on the plan. A paved area is 12.8 cm × 2.8 cm. What is total for both areas, in square metres?

Answer:

_____

QUESTION 8

A grassed area on the plan measures 6.9 cm × 6.2 cm. The area is adjacent to a garden bed that measures 6.2 cm × 0.9 cm and a paved area that borders the garden that is 6.2 cm × 0.7 cm.

a   What is the total for the three areas, in square metres?

Answer:

_____

b   If there are 42 pavers per m², how many pavers are needed?

Answer:

_____

QUESTION 9

An area for annuals measures 7.7 cm × 2.3 cm. A paved area measures 7.7 cm × 3.4 cm, and an area for a vegetable garden measures 3.4 cm × 3.2 cm.

a   What is the total area?

Answer:

_____

b   How many pavers are needed if there are 28 pavers per m²?

Answer:

_____

QUESTION 10

An area is designed for a sculpture that measures 1.8 cm × 1.8 cm, a flower bed that measures 5.5 cm × 2.8 cm, a vegetable garden that measures 4.8 cm × 1.2 cm, a patio area that measures 3.8 cm × 3.8 cm, a spa area that measures 2.3 cm × 2.3 cm, and an open grassed area that measures 5.3 cm × 5.8 cm. What is the total area, in square metres?

Answer:

_____

Section E: Planting groundcover, bulbs and shrubs

Short-answer questions

Specific instructions to students

- This section is designed to help you to improve your Maths skills in the horticulture trade.
- Read the questions below and answer all of them in the spaces provided.
- You may not use a calculator.
- You need to show all working.
- Reduce the ratios to the simplest or lowest form.

QUESTION 1

A client wants a garden bed that is 6 m × 2 m to be prepared for groundcover plants. The groundcover plants being planted are Beacon Silver (*Lamium maculatum*). The planting density is three plants per square metre.

a   How many plants are needed?

Answer:

_____

b   If each plant costs $11.15, what is the cost for the plants?

Answer:

_____

QUESTION 2

Alamy / Alex Ramsay

A client discusses with a landscaper that they want to mass-plant a particular groundcover plant, *Convolvulus cneorum*, in eight garden beds that are 9 m × 3 m, and which will contain rock features. The planting density is three plants per square metre.

a   How many plants are needed for each bed?

Answer:

_____

b   How many plants are needed for all eight garden beds?

Answer:

_____

c   If each plant costs $17.48, what is the total cost for all of the plants?

Answer:

_____

QUESTION 3

The client, who is the director of a retirement village, works with a horticulture assistant to plan the planting of groundcover in 15 areas across the village. The client wants to mass-plant Parrot's Beak Lotus (*Lotus berthelotii*) in each 4.6 m × 3.5 m area. The planting density is three plants per square metre.

a   How many plants are needed for each area?

Answer:

_____

b   How many plants are needed for all 15 areas?

Answer:

_____

c   If each plant costs $8.98, what is the total cost for all of the plants?

Answer:

_____

QUESTION 4

A horticulture assistant consults with a client and they decide together that they will plant tuberose bulbs (*Polianthes tuberosa*), as they are known to emanate an intense, sweet scent. The four bulbs are bought for $20.60. How much does each bulb cost?

Answer:

_____

QUESTION 5

In Australia, the best time to plant spring flowering bulbs is between April and May. A horticulture assistant talks with the client and her supervisor and they decide to plant Agapanthus. They buy 25 bulbs for $62.50. How much does each bulb cost?

Answer:

_____

QUESTION 6

A gardener, an assistant gardener and a client discuss what type of bulbs will be planted. They settle on Brindisi bulbs (*Lilium asiatic*). They need 15 bulbs, which come to a total cost of $13.11. How much does each bulb cost?

Answer:

_____

QUESTION 7

A gardener talks with the supervisor after they have both carried out a visual inspection of a park. They decide to plant the native Australian shrub Kanooka Water Gum (*Tristaniopsis laurina*). It grows to a height of 8 m with a 6 m canopy, and will tolerate a range of soils including well-drained rocky soils and heavy clay loams, as long as sufficient water is available. The price of a 400-m/45-L shrub is $58.75. A total of 23 need to be purchased. What is the total cost?

Answer:

QUESTION 8

A horticulture worker and a supervisor discuss the need to plant native shrubs across a park. They decide to plant the native Australian shrub White Ash (*Fraxinus americana*). They decide on this shrub because it grows to a maximum height of 11 m with a maximum canopy of 8 m. It is also known to be a symmetrical and hardy tree that will provide sufficient shade in the summer. This is important because there needs to be shaded areas in the park. They purchase 16 100-L plants at $121.50 each, on special, from a nursery. What is the total cost?

Answer:

QUESTION 9

Oak trees are being considered by a council for mass-planting in local streets. The horticulturalist advises the council to plant an oak that is resistant to pests, is hardy, is tolerant of dry conditions and has vigorous growth. Pin Oak trees (*Quercus palustris*) are selected. They purchase 32 100-L trees from a nursery at a unit cost of $315.50. What is the total cost?

Answer:

QUESTION 10

A deciduous, wide-crowned tree is being considered for planting in an inland park. The horticulturalist thinks it will be best to have a plant that likes full sun, rich soil and regular watering. It is also important that the plant is tolerant of hot, dry conditions and alkaline soils. It is decided that Golden Rain trees (*Koelreuteria paniculata*) are the best plant for the area. They purchase 11 75-L trees at $264.75 each. What is the total cost for the trees?

Answer:

9780170473385

Horticulture
Practice Written Exam for the Horticulture Trade

Reading time: 10 minutes
Writing time: 1 hour 30 minutes

Section A: Literacy
Section B: General Mathematics
Section C: Trade Mathematics

QUESTION and ANSWER BOOK

Section	Topic	Number of questions	Marks
A	Literacy	7	22
B	General Mathematics	11	26
C	Trade Mathematics	48	52
		Total 66	Total 100

The sections may be completed in the order of your choice.
NO CALCULATORS are to be used during the exam.

Spelling

Read the passage below and then underline the 20 spelling errors.

10 marks

A number of plants are known to have arommatic leaves or stems, which releace fragrunce when touched. These types of plants can be planted close to walking paths in an efort to release the arroma when someone walks by. Certain plants can provide food, such as nectar, fruit, beries or seeds, which might atract birds to them so as to help with the pollination process.

Many gardens across Australia relly on bore water to sarvive. The quality of bore water may vary considerably at different geographical locations. Some bore water tends to be highly mineralised and salts have a tendancy to build up in soils and then they may become toxik to particular plants. In many cases, it is a good idea to switch between bore water and another water source that is available in the same area.

A type of insect that is attracted to gardens is the buterfly. Many butterflies tend to be attracted to certain plants that provide food for catapillars and nectar for the adalt butterflies. Specific butterfly spesies feed on a certain type of food plant. A range of vegatables and fruit-producing plants are a good idea for many gardens. Food plants require regalar watering, which can be a probblem as they are not considered to be water-wise.

Causion should always be taken when considering whether a plant is edible or not. Many people are unaware that some well-known food plants, such as variaties of rhubarb and potatoes, can be poisonous if they are eaten raw.

Correct the spelling errors by writing them out with the correct spelling below.

_____

_____

Alphabetising

Put the following words into alphabetical order.

7 marks

Potting mix	Safety goggles
Cottage plants	Liquid fertiliser
Annual	Safety boots
Water-wise	Gloves
Mulch	Hanging basket
Cuttings	Secateurs
Perennial	Plants

_____

_____

_____

_____

_____

_____

_____

_____

_____

_____

_____

_____

_____

_____

Comprehension

Short-answer questions

Specific instructions to students

- Read the passage and then answer the questions that follow.

Peggy is a landscape gardener. She contemplates planning a garden and is considering a range of different plants and trees, particularly evergreen, deciduous and semi-deciduous trees. Peggy knows that evergreen trees are best recognised as a tree that retains its leaves throughout the year. The density of the tree may fall slightly during dry or cool weather; however, this is generally not noticeable. Another type of tree is the deciduous tree, which drops all of its leaves during the cooler parts of the year. This is a form of protection from the damage that cold can cause. As the days shorten during autumn, the tree begins to lose its leaves.

Autumn is often associated with remarkable displays of leaf colour from a range of trees and plants. Deciduous plants are indicative of temperate zones and limited deciduous plants will grow in warmer zones. Plants such as semi-deciduous plants tend to drop most or all of their leaves due to conditions such as drought, so as to conserve water over the dryer months. Factors such as season, climate and the levels of moisture in the soil may contribute to leaf-drop. Semi-deciduous plants are most noted in subtropical and tropical areas.

QUESTION 1   1 mark

What are the three particular types of tree that Peggy is considering for her garden?

Answer:

_____

_____

QUESTION 2   1 mark

Why does the density of a tree change?

Answer:

_____

_____

QUESTION 3   1 mark

What are deciduous trees and what do they do when seasons change?

Answer:

_____

_____

QUESTION 4   1 mark

Why do semi-deciduous trees lose their leaves?

Answer:

_____

_____

_____

QUESTION 5   1 mark

What are the factors that contribute to leaf-drop?

Answer:

_____

_____

Section B: General Mathematics

QUESTION 1   1+1+1 = 3 marks

What unit of measurement would you use to measure:

a   the length of edging along a garden?

Answer:

_____

b   the height of a tree?

Answer:

_____

c   the amount of mulch used in a garden?

Answer:

_____

QUESTION 2   1+1+1 = 3 marks

Give examples of how the following might be used in the horticultural trade.

a   Percentage

Answer:

_____

b   Decimals

Answer:

_____

c   Fraction

Answer:

_____

QUESTION 3   1+1 = 2 marks

Convert the following units.

a   1 kg to grams

Answer:

_____

b   1500 g to kilograms

Answer:

_____

QUESTION 4   2 marks

Write the following in descending order.

0.7   0.71   7.1   70.1   701.00   7.0

Answer:

_____

QUESTION 5   1+1 = 2 marks

Write the decimal number that is between:

a   0.1 and 0.2

Answer:

_____

b   1.3 and 1.4

Answer:

_____

QUESTION 6   1+1 = 2 marks

Round off the following numbers to two (2) decimal places.

a   5.177

Answer:

_____

b   12.655

Answer:

_____

QUESTION 7   1+1 = 2 marks

Estimate the following by approximation.

a 101×81

Answer:

_____

b 399×21

Answer:

_____

QUESTION 8   1+1 = 2 marks

What do the following add up to?

a $25, $13.50 and $165.50

Answer:

b $4, $5.99 and $229.50

Answer:

QUESTION 9   1+1 = 2 marks

Subtract the following.

a 196 from 813

Answer:

b 5556 from 9223

Answer:

QUESTION 10   1+1 = 2 marks

Use division to solve the following.

a $4824 \div 3 =$

Answer:

b $84.2 \div 0.4 =$

Answer:

QUESTION 11   2+2 = 4 marks

Using BODMAS, solve the following.

a $(3 \times 7) \times 4 + 9 - 5 =$

Answer:

b $(8 \times 12) \times 2 + 8 - 4 =$

Answer:

Section C: Trade Mathematics

Basic Operations

Addition

QUESTION 1   1 mark

A landscape company purchases 36 bags of pine bark mulch, 144 perennial plants and 15 stakes for plants. How many items have been purchased in total?

Answer:

QUESTION 2   1 mark

Three gardening tools are purchased for $25, $45 and $17. What is the total cost?

Answer:

Subtraction

QUESTION 1   1 mark

A nursery worker uses 57 cable ties from a box that contains 150 cable ties. How many remain?

Answer:

QUESTION 2   1 mark

A gardener purchases personal protective equipment (PPE) and the total comes to $124. The manager of the shop takes off a discount of $35 during a sale. How much does the gardener pay?

Answer:

Multiplication

QUESTION 1   1 mark

Seven bottles of 750-mL insect killer are used over the course of one day. If one bottle costs $8, how much do seven bottles cost?

Answer:

_____

QUESTION 2   1 mark

A gardener purchases six 250-mm Amethyst Falls Wisteria for $34 each, two 270-mm sweet viburnum (*Viburnum odoratissimum*) for $35 each, and four *Nandina domestica 'Nana'* for $38 each. What is the total cost?

Answer:

_____

Division

QUESTION 1   1 mark

An invoice for a landscaping job comes to $5578, which is the cost for completing a redesign of a major landscape at a winery. If the work took six days to complete, what is the average cost per day?

Answer:

_____

QUESTION 2   1 mark

At a yearly stocktake, a gardener counts 72 bags of 50-L pine bark mulch. If 12 bags are packed onto each pallet, how many pallets are there?

Answer:

_____

Decimals

Addition

QUESTION 1   1 mark

A customer buys a 40-g packet of caterpillar killer for $19.95, a 750-mL spray bottle of pyrethrum for $9.50 and a 200-mL bottle of fruit fly control for $24.50. How much is charged for the purchase?

Answer:

_____

QUESTION 2   1 mark

During a sale, a garden nursery sells a spark plug for a mower for $7.95, a mower blade and bolt set for $11.50 and a foam air filter element for $12.85. What is the total for all three items?

Answer:

_____

Subtraction

QUESTION 1   1 mark

A casual labourer earns $418.50 for two days of work. He spends $35.95 on clothes and $25.50 on food? How much money does he have left?

Answer:

_____

QUESTION 2   1 mark

A nursery manager purchases two push lawn mowers for $124.50. If she pays for them with three $50 notes from the float, how much change is given?

Answer:

_____

Multiplication

QUESTION 1   2 marks

A customer buys three 1-L bottles of four-stoke oil, valued at $12.95 each.

a   How much does it cost for the three bottles?

Answer:

_____

b   How much change is given from $50.00?

Answer:

_____

QUESTION 2   2 marks

Four hedge shearers are purchased at a cost of $28.50 each.

a   What is the total cost?

Answer:

_____

b   How much change is given from $120.00?

Answer:

_____

Division

QUESTION 1   1 mark

A nursery manager earns $987.00 for five days of work. How much is earned per day?

Answer:

_____

QUESTION 2   1 mark

Four 10-kg bags of complete 'D' granular fertiliser are purchased from a gardening store. The total for all four bags comes to $88.80. What is the cost per bag?

Answer:

_____

Fractions

QUESTION 1   1 mark

$\frac{1}{4} + \frac{1}{2} =$

Answer:

_____

QUESTION 2   1 mark

$\frac{4}{5} - \frac{1}{3} =$

Answer:

_____

QUESTION 3   1 mark

$\frac{2}{3} \times \frac{1}{4} =$

Answer:

_____

QUESTION 4   1 mark

$\frac{3}{4} \div \frac{1}{2} =$

Answer:

_____

Percentages

QUESTION 1   1 mark

A garden nursery has a '10% off' sale on all items. A customer purchases items for $149.00. What is the final sale price after the discount has been given?

Answer:

_____

QUESTION 2   1 mark

PPE gear used for landscaping and outdoor work is discounted by 20% in a store. If the regular retail price of the gear comes to $120.00, how much does the customer pay after the discount?

Answer:

_____

Measurement Conversions

QUESTION 1   1 mark

How many grams are in 1.85 kg?

Answer:

_____

QUESTION 2   1 mark

How many centimetres are in 35 mm?

Answer:

_____

Measurement – Area, Perimeter and Volume

Area

QUESTION 1   1 mark

The surface area of a rectangular garden bed measures 15 m × 6 m. What is the total floor area?

Answer:

_____

QUESTION 2   1 mark

What is the total area of a vegetable garden that measures 2.2 m × 1.5 m?

Answer:

_____

Perimeter

QUESTION 1   1 mark

Calculate the perimeter of a lawn that is 12 m long × 7 m wide.

Answer:

_____

QUESTION 2   1 mark

Pavers are being laid around the perimeter of a garden that measures 3.8 m × 1.7 m. What is the length of the perimeter?

Answer:

_____

Volume of a rectangle

QUESTION 1   1 mark

A 6 × 4 trailer is being used to transport loam soil for a garden that measures 6 m × 2 m × 0.1 m. How many cubic metres of soil are needed?

Answer:

_____

QUESTION 2   1 mark

Play-grade bark is needed to cover a play area in a park that measures 15 m × 15 m × 300 mm. How many cubic metres of bark are required?

Answer:

_____

Volume of a circle

QUESTION 1   1 mark

A circular pond has a radius of 1 m across and is 0.5 m deep. What is the volume of water of the pond, in cubic metres?

Answer:

_____

QUESTION 2   1 mark

Two garden beds are both semi-circular shaped and each has a diameter of 4 m. If soil needs to be added to a depth of 0.2 m, how much soil is needed for both garden beds, in cubic metres?

Answer:

_____

Time, Motion and Money

QUESTION 1   1 mark

A casual junior gardener is paid $12.50 per hour. If she works for 15 hours over two days, how much is her gross pay?

Answer:

_____

QUESTION 2   2 marks

A horticulturalist spends the following amount of time on tasks: 17 minutes, 35 minutes, 19 minutes, 48 minutes and 58 minutes.

a   How many minutes were used to complete the tasks?

Answer:

_____

b   How much time was taken in hours and minutes?

Answer:

_____

Squaring Numbers

QUESTION 1   1 mark

What is 7^2?

Answer:

_____

QUESTION 2   1 mark

One area of a nursery measures $13\,m \times 13\,m$. What is the total area for the nursery?

Answer:

_____

Ratios

QUESTION 1   1 mark

To make up a two-stroke mix for a weed trimmer, a gardener needs to use a ratio of 25 : 1 fuel to oil mix. How much oil is added to 10 L of fuel?

Answer:

_____

QUESTION 2   1 mark

A chainsaw uses two-stroke fuel in the ratio of 50 : 1 fuel to oil. How much oil needs to be mixed to 5 L of fuel?

Answer:

_____

Applying Maths to the Horticulture Trade

Wages

QUESTION 1   1 mark

A landscape gardener earns $25.50 per hour and works for 38 hours over a week. How much does she earn before tax?

Answer:

_____

QUESTION 2   1 mark

A nursery manager gets paid $26.75 per hour. He works for 38 hours per week and gets paid weekly. If he spends $45.50 on petrol, $49.50 on food and $67.75 on entertainment, how much money does he have left over?

Answer:

_____

Flow rates and chemicals

QUESTION 1   1 mark

The tank on a backpack sprayer holds 10 litres.
If the sprayer has a flow rate of 1.25 litres per
minute, approximately how long will it take for the
sprayer to run out?

Answer:

_____

QUESTION 2   1 mark

Aphids and caterpillars have infested a garden and
need to be controlled. A natural solution of soap flakes
and water is made up and added to a 10-L backpack
sprayer. The spray rate is 2.5 litres per minute. How
long will the solution last?

Answer:

_____

Spray time

QUESTION 1   1 mark

A ground application rate of 10 mL of insecticide per
100 L of water is needed. If a spraying pack holds 10 L,
how much insecticide needs to be added to the water?

Answer:

_____

QUESTION 2   1 mark

A vegetable grower decides to use an application rate
of 200 ml of insecticide per 250 L of water. The spraying
backpack holds 10 L. How much insecticide needs to be
added to the water?

Answer:

_____

Planning a garden landscape

QUESTION 1   1 mark

If the fence measures 18 cm on a map and the map has
a 1 : 100 scale, how many metres is the fence in reality?

Answer:

_____

QUESTION 2   1 mark

A garden bed measures 12.8 cm × 1.2 cm on a landscape
plan that has 1 : 100 scale. Calculate the area in metres.

Answer:

_____

Planting groundcover, bulbs and shrubs

QUESTION 1   1 mark

Twenty bulbs are bought for a total of $60.80. How
much does each bulb cost?

Answer:

_____

QUESTION 2   2 marks

A client wants a garden bed that is 8 m × 2 m, to plant
groundcover plants. If the plant density is three plants
per m^2, how many plants are needed?

Answer:

_____

Glossary

Acid soils   Acid soils have a pH reading of less than 6.5. The majority of Australian soils are considered acidic and can be improved by adding dolomite or lime.

Aerobic   A method of composting that is driven by organisms that require oxygen.

Alkaline soils   Alkaline soils have a pH reading of 7.4 and above and are known to contain relatively high amounts of lime. Alkaline soils can be improved by adding sulphur and organic matter.

Anaerobic   A method of composting that is driven by organisms that thrive when oxygen is limited or virtually non-existent.

Arborist   A specialist who cares for and maintains trees, which may include planting, pruning, and identifying and treating trees that might be distressed or considered to be in poor health.

Bulb   Bulbs are generally perennial and resemble large buds wrapped with overlapping leaf-like scales. These leaf-like scales provide food to the plant as it grows.

Backfilling   The process of replacing soil excavated from a planting hole after planting.

Compost   This material can be made from decomposed garden and food waste or obtained from gardening outlets in a ready-to-use form.

Cutting   A section of a root, stem, or leaf that is used to propagate a new plant complete with its own roots.

Deciduous   Trees and shrubs that shed all of their leaves during the resting period of their growth.

Espalier   The process of training a tree or shrub to grow flat against a wall or fence.

Evergreens   Plants that retain their leaves virtually all year

Grafting   The process of joining the stem (cutting) of one plant to another. This is usually done to create a stronger or more desirable plant.

Grey water   This type of water generally comes from sources such as sinks, baths, washing machines and showers. Grey water may comprise green cleaners. It is usually free of fats and oils and may be used treated or untreated in many areas of horticulture.

Gypsum   This substance has the ability to add calcium to the soil thus decreasing the possibility of blossom end rot. Gypsum can improve the arrangement and workability of many clay and saline soils.

Herbaceous   Soft-stemmed perennial plants

Micronutrients   These nutrients are essential, in minute amounts, for plant health. Most Australian soils are deficient in iodine, selenium and boron.

Mulch   Organic material, such as straw, Lucerne, bark or compost, which is spread over a surface to conserve moisture and deter weed growth. Inorganic mulches, such as pebbles, gravel and sand can also be used.

Organic   This term refers to fertilisers, chemicals and products that are or have been alive at some stage. This term is also used for gardening when using no artificial fertilisers or pesticides.

pH   pH stands for 'potency of hydrogen'. A pH kit can be used to measure acidity or alkalinity levels in soil, compost or water. Water has a pH reading of 7, which is considered neutral. See also alkaline soils and acid soils.

Seedbed   A garden bed that has been prepared for raising seeds. Preparation involves removal of weeds, rocks and lumps of soil.

Slow-release fertiliser   A fertiliser that releases nutrients gradually over a period of time.

9780170473385

Formulae and Data

Area

$Area = l \times b$

Area = length $\times$ breadth and is given in square units

Perimeter

Perimeter is the length of all sides added together.

Perimeter = length + breadth + length + breadth

Volume = $l + b + l + b$

Volume of a rectangle

Volume = length $\times$ width $\times$ height and is given in cubic units

Volume = $l \times w \times h$

Volume of a circle

Volume of a circle = pi $\times$ radius squared $\times$ by height/depth and is given in cubic units

Volume = $\pi \times r^2 \times h$

Times Tables

1	**2**	**3**	**4**
1 × 1 = 1	1 × 2 = 2	1 × 3 = 3	1 × 4 = 4
2 × 1 = 2	2 × 2 = 4	2 × 3 = 6	2 × 4 = 8
3 × 1 = 3	3 × 2 = 6	3 × 3 = 9	3 × 4 = 12
4 × 1 = 4	4 × 2 = 8	4 × 3 = 12	4 × 4 = 16
5 × 1 = 5	5 × 2 = 10	5 × 3 = 15	5 × 4 = 20
6 × 1 = 6	6 × 2 = 12	6 × 3 = 18	6 × 4 = 24
7 × 1 = 7	7 × 2 = 14	7 × 3 = 21	7 × 4 = 28
8 × 1 = 8	8 × 2 = 16	8 × 3 = 24	8 × 4 = 32
9 × 1 = 9	9 × 2 = 18	9 × 3 = 27	9 × 4 = 36
10 × 1 = 10	10 × 2 = 20	10 × 3 = 30	10 × 4 = 40
11 × 1 = 11	11 × 2 = 22	11 × 3 = 33	11 × 4 = 44
12 × 1 = 12	12 × 2 = 24	12 × 3 = 36	12 × 4 = 48

5	**6**	**7**	**8**
1 × 5 = 5	1 × 6 = 6	1 × 7 = 7	1 × 8 = 8
2 × 5 = 10	2 × 6 = 12	2 × 7 = 14	2 × 8 = 16
3 × 5 = 15	3 × 6 = 18	3 × 7 = 21	3 × 8 = 24
4 × 5 = 20	4 × 6 = 24	4 × 7 = 28	4 × 8 = 32
5 × 5 = 25	5 × 6 = 30	5 × 7 = 35	5 × 8 = 40
6 × 5 = 30	6 × 6 = 36	6 × 7 = 42	6 × 8 = 48
7 × 5 = 35	7 × 6 = 42	7 × 7 = 49	7 × 8 = 56
8 × 5 = 40	8 × 6 = 48	8 × 7 = 56	8 × 8 = 64
9 × 5 = 45	9 × 6 = 54	9 × 7 = 63	9 × 8 = 72
10 × 5 = 50	10 × 6 = 60	10 × 7 = 70	10 × 8 = 80
11 × 5 = 55	11 × 6 = 66	11 × 7 = 77	11 × 8 = 88
12 × 5 = 60	12 × 6 = 72	12 × 7 = 84	12 × 8 = 96

9	**10**	**11**	**12**
1 × 9 = 9	1 × 10 = 10	1 × 11 = 11	1 × 12 = 12
2 × 9 = 18	2 × 10 = 20	2 × 11 = 22	2 × 12 = 24
3 × 9 = 27	3 × 10 = 30	3 × 11 = 33	3 × 12 = 36
4 × 9 = 36	4 × 10 = 40	4 × 11 = 44	4 × 12 = 48
5 × 9 = 45	5 × 10 = 50	5 × 11 = 55	5 × 12 = 60
6 × 9 = 54	6 × 10 = 60	6 × 11 = 66	6 × 12 = 72
7 × 9 = 63	7 × 10 = 70	7 × 11 = 77	7 × 12 = 84
8 × 9 = 72	8 × 10 = 80	8 × 11 = 88	8 × 12 = 96
9 × 9 = 81	9 × 10 = 90	9 × 11 = 99	9 × 12 = 108
10 × 9 = 90	10 × 10 = 100	10 × 11 = 110	10 × 12 = 120
11 × 9 = 99	11 × 10 = 110	11 × 11 = 121	11 × 12 = 132
12 × 9 = 108	12 × 10 = 120	12 × 11 = 132	12 × 12 = 144

9780170473385

Multiplication Grid

×	1	2	3	4	5	6	7	8	9	10	11	12
1	1	2	3	4	5	6	7	8	9	10	11	12
2	2	4	6	8	10	12	14	16	18	20	22	24
3	3	6	9	12	15	18	21	24	27	30	33	36
4	4	8	12	16	20	24	28	32	36	40	44	48
5	5	10	15	20	25	30	35	40	45	50	55	60
6	6	12	18	24	30	36	42	48	54	60	66	72
7	7	14	21	28	35	42	49	56	63	70	77	84
8	8	16	24	32	40	48	56	64	72	80	88	96
9	9	18	27	36	45	54	63	72	81	90	99	108
10	10	20	30	40	50	60	70	80	90	100	110	120
11	11	22	33	44	55	66	77	88	99	110	121	132
12	12	24	36	48	60	72	84	96	108	120	132	144

Notes

Notes

Notes

Notes

Notes